A PH.D.'S GUIDE TO WINNING AT THE RACES

by

Dr. Jeffry Weiss

INDEX

INTRODUCTION

This book is not simply about racetrack betting. It is about regaining control of your life. There is no such thing as a "career job" anymore. The average person has 6 jobs during their lifetime. When a person is let go, the average salary at their new position is 67% of their old salary.

Companies today want more than your time. They want you to consider your job over your health and the welfare of your family. After all, there are a dozen more people standing in line to take your place should you not be deemed a "team player."

With the constantly changing nature of business and technology, the only guarantee is that there are no guarantees. Change is the only certainty, and whether you will be on the forefront of that change or swept aside by it is just as much luck as it is due diligence. You can either help someone or some company achieve success, or attain lasting successful for yourself. They are, very often, mutually exclusive.

There are those who seek their independence by starting their own business.

This has a number of inherent problems. First, it takes money. The average worker spends 101.5% of their income each year. That means he or she is constantly going deeper into debt; hardly a scenario that leads to saving enough money to begin a business. Second, statistics show that almost all businesses are under funded. That means it takes more money than projected at the start. How much more? Between three and four times. Third, self-employed people work an average of 65 hours a week compared to 45 hours per week for those employed at regular jobs. Fourth, almost every self-employed person I have met said that if they knew how hard it was going to be to start their own business, they would never have undertaken the task.

So, are there businesses that can provide added income, or even provide financial independence without demanding a total commitment of money and time?

Before I answer that, allow me to introduce myself. I am Dr. Jeffry Weiss. My formal education took place at Drexel University (B.S. - Accounting), Temple University (M.B.A. – Statistical Analysis), The University of Pennsylvania (M.A. - International Affairs), Clayton College – (Ph.D. - Mathematics).

I was a stock market analyst and investor, and put out my own mutual fund newsletter. I was a day trader for five years. I owned a car dealership. I helped found a natural food business. I have been a freelance writer for 33 years. I invested in real estate. And I developed a number of Internet businesses.

6

Most of these businesses were relatively successful, but they all had something else in common. They demanded so much of my time and energy that I didn't have a life. My definition of success is having the time and energy to enjoy the fruits of your labor. And so I dedicated two decades to discovering alternatives to the nine to five routine: two days off per week, two weeks off per year.

I sought out business opportunities that could not only make me money, but also allow me the time and energy to share with my friends and family and provide for them as I had always hoped. I was led to horse racing because a very astute friend of mine felt I could use my skills in statistics and risk analysis to help him devise a system to beat the races.

I started out as a handicapper: using all the information about the past performances of horses to determine their perspective chances. Yet things were far different in those days. I had to drive to the racetrack – sometimes hours away, and I had to stay all day to find even one potential bet. It was a full time job. Racetracks were not around the corner; in fact if you wanted to bet all year round, you had to physically move with the end of each racing season.

You couldn't hold a full time job unless you were a night watchman and could sleep on the job. And there were inherent expenses. Before I placed my first bet, I was down twenty or more dollars (gas, program, racing form, lunch, admission fee) – a lot of money twenty years ago. Also, in those days, I was limited to the opportunities at hand. There were good, sometimes better, bets at other racetracks, but I couldn't be at two places at once.

While it used to be that your presence was required at the racetrack, betting now can be accomplished from the comfort of your own home or office. This opens up new realms of possibilities. Pari-mutual wagering is now available in every state, and the only expense is the Daily Racing Form. This you get on line. And you don't have to download the entire paper, only the three or four races that qualify each day. The cost of that will be $299 for the entire year. No other costs are involved. It is no longer necessary to travel to the racetrack, spend money on gas, entrance fees, and food.

With the advent of off-track betting, and now Internet betting, the advantages are many. You can bet while you are working, you can make it your primary source of income or a supplement to your current wages. You can bet from your computer at work or at home, or if computer use is monitored, you can bet via your cell phone.

WHY THIS BOOK . . . WHY NOW

A series of recent events led me to write this book. I had many close friends lose their high-tech jobs in the dot.com crash. When they tried to find new jobs, they were offered an average of one-third their previous salaries.

When we met they all shared their frustrations. It hurt me to see the people I loved have their lives so adversely affected. We spoke about situations that might enable them to not be at the mercy of technology or the whims of the economy. We talked about the success I had had as a handicapper. They were all excited by the possibility of having that much freedom, and of being able to supplement their income by pari-mutuel wagering.

It all sounded good, however I explained to them that when I went to the track, I kept all the information in my head. I hadn't needed to put it down on paper. What they were asking was a quantum leap in ability. There are thousands of statistics involved in handicapping. To synthesize that down to a few manageable steps that could be undertaken in a few moments would be a formidable task.

But this wasn't just for me. It wasn't some theoretical game. The economic security of close friends was at stake. I had accumulated year's worth of Daily Racing Forms with the past performances of all the horses at the major tracks and the outcomes of all those races. It took me three years to put the system together. I checked it at every major track. The results were almost precisely as I expected. With a bankroll of $1000, wagering an average of 12% of your capital on each betable race, the win percentage is 75%. We have found an average of one bet every two days when looking at seven race tracks per day. Now that not be spectacular to you, but that's $580 per month with a $1000 bankroll. And it requires only minutes a day!

How much time will this system takes to implement each day? That is key question for those with very limited time and many responsibilities. After a brief period learning how to read the Racing Form, it will take only twenty to thirty minutes a per day. That is based on numerous people already using this proven system. Your time may vary but only by minutes.

This system may not make you rich, but it does provide added income to those seeking greater opportunity. And it can provide a living for those whose life style is not lavish. But there are limitations. You cannot bet more than 12% of your money in any one race (excluding our incremental variant which will be discussed later). To bet more than 12%, risks your bankroll, and means that you are not considering losing streaks, although they are normally short in duration. You must be patient and in control. You cannot deviate from the system. Now that may seem easy, but as one accumulates knowledge it is easy to think you have some insight into the handicapping process. But this isn't about handicapping; it's about using irrefutable statistics to insure a fixed return.

Why don't I play my own system and get rich? My calling is as a writer and researcher. Writing allows me to reach millions of people. I have developed a totally new approach to overcoming obesity in our country. My dream has been to make a real difference in the world.

Yet there are many ways to make a difference. My accumulated knowledge can be applied in a number of directions and a broad spectrum of disciplines.

Writing this book was an enormous challenge. I had to synthesize all my knowledge of handicapping and betting into just a few concise rules. I had to take thirty years of knowledge and compress what I had learned into a single, small, readable book. The system on the following pages may seem eminently simple, but it's based on decades of study. Now before we focus on the rules, let's take in a little history of pari-mutual wagering.

THE EVOLUTION OF BETTING

This is more than a philosophic discussion. Recognition and appreciation of how betting evolved and the psychology of betting can give us the necessary awareness of how emotions lead to losses and how you can maintain a clear edge over less informed bettors.The exact date is unknown, lost in the mist of time. One prehistoric man astride an animal raced another to see whose beast of burden was fastest. You can be certain that someone was betting on one or the other and was probably laying odds.

Since that time man has been fascinated by the prospect of pitting creatures with speed and skill against each other. In the Athens of Pericles it was man against man, matching speed, endurance, and agility in the first Olympic Games. In Imperial Rome, the contest was a savage struggle between teams of horses pulling chariot and driver.

Whenever and wherever there was a contest of speed, you can be sure at least two men had money on it.

And at some time an enterprising man recognized that, by handling all the bets on a given contest with suitable adjustments in the

14

odds, he could turn a steady profit with virtually no risk. Thus the first handbook was born. Progress from that unsung genius to the modern racetrack with its electronic tote board was just a matter of time.

As racing has grown in popularity, it has become steadily more organized, and the planning and operation of race meets has grown both more businesslike and more scientific. But the average bettor still flounders along playing hunches, plunging on "sure things," and blaming bad luck for his daily financial beatings. There is nothing scientific or businesslike in the way he selects his horses or makes his bets. He is usually laboring under several misconceptions about racing; to make matters worse, he is deluged with systems, tips, inside information, and other sure-win claims, until his head reels. Even when he manages to pick a winner or two, he rarely takes any money home unless he wins the last race of the day.

If the description above fits you, don't be too upset. It fits 95 percent of all horseplayers. What about the other five percent? What magic trick do they have? Virtually all of them treat race betting as a business, using sound logic, organized handicapping, and careful money management to insure a steady return on their investments. This book is designed to teach you how to join the ranks of this blessed five percent.

This book has three primary objectives. First, to dispel the clouds of mystery and misinformation that have surrounded the sport and business of thoroughbred racing. Second, to share with the reader the knowledge gained from years of study and participation. Third, and most important, to compile and organize this knowledge into a workable and logical method of handicapping and betting that, together with sound money management, can bring profits and success to anyone. Anyone, that is, with self-control, discipline, and determination.

You will think and act like a professional, a businessman if you will. You will utilize the law of averages . . . in the final analysis the horseplayer's best friend.

Above all, you will know what you are doing and why you are doing it. You will be able to enjoy casual wagering as a novice or wealth and independence as a 'professional' by using formulas suitable for the amount of capital you have.

THE STOCK MARKET VS. PARI-MUTUAL WAGERING

I have been asked to compare investing in the stock market to pari-mutual wagering. I have studied the stock market from both a technical and fundamental standpoint. So, with equal experience, why am I advocating the racetrack as the better "investment?" It all comes down to who you are betting against – at both the racetrack and in the stock market, you are betting against someone else. For every person who sells a stock, someone must be buying. That is the job of the market makers: balancing out buy orders with sell orders to maintain an orderly, balanced market. The smarter your adversary, the more difficult it is to make money. The term "rocket scientist" was coined in regards to the people who invest in the stock market. The greatest minds have always gravitated to the stock market.

At the racetrack, the odds are established when people choose different horses. You are betting against other bettors, not against the racetrack. And those other bettors are not trained in statistical analysis; nor are they able to act unemotionally or stick to any one method of selecting or betting horses. So why do so many more people seek out the stock market rather than easier investment medium? Maybe because it offers the greatest challenge. Maybe because it is considered "socially acceptable." Maybe because people who "invest" in the market wear suits and ties. Regardless of the reasons, I can assure you that making money in the stock market is far more difficult than making money at the racetrack. To answer the question, "Is it possible to win at the races? Yes. Actually, it is relatively easy. After all you are not playing against rocket scientists.

FUNDAMENTAL VS. TECHNICAL ANALYSIS

The terms "fundamental" and "technical" analysis" are borrowed from the stock market and can be applied quite directly to racetrack betting. A fundamental analyst, in Wall Street jargon, is someone who studies the real underlying factors that are likely to determine the future success or failure of prospective investments - for example, the quality of a company's management, the growth potential of its major markets, and the abilities of its corporate rivals. The purpose of such study is to determine whether the company in question is a "good" investment.

In contrast, the technical analyst (sometimes known as a "chartist") tends to ignore the fundamentals, focusing instead on the behavior of the prices of prospective investments. The technician does not neces-sarily claim that fundamentals don't matter. Rather, the argument goes, one need not study the fundamentals, because they tend already to be reflected in the prices of the investment possibilities. In other words, information about the investment prospects can be gleaned simply from studying the recent history of their market prices; and certain patterns of price behavior point to propitious investments.

The analogy with horse racing is reasonably close, if not precise. Certain fundamental factors, such as the speed and condition of rival horses, determine their winning probabilities. The study of such factors may therefore reveal which horse is most likely to win a particular race; this analysis in turn may suggest which is a "good" bet.

Technical analysis of horse racing, in contrast, focuses on the "price" - that is, the betting odds - of the various horses. Is a particular horse a very fast runner? "Fine," the technician will say, "this information no doubt has been recognized by bettors, and is already 'in' this horse's price in the form of relatively low betting odds on the animal." As in the stock market case, certain odds (prices) may suggest a "good" bet.

The truth is, however, it is possible to be a relatively successful racetrack gambler without knowing a great deal about horses or racing. (Not terribly surprising when you consider that after all, you may be a very good driver without understanding the internal combustion engine or a competent user of standard computer programs without really knowing how computers work.). In fact, ultimately we will argue that the most effective verifiable betting strategies do not require a great deal of expertise about the horses themselves.

We may ask whether one can make consistently above-average profits in racetrack betting. Now we already know that in the aggregate, racetrack betting is a losing proposition: Since the track takes out about 18 percent of all moneys bet, bettors as a whole experience a substantial negative return. But can one make profits much above this average by betting on particular horses? Since the average return is minus 18 percent, even break-ing even in the long run would seem to be a substantial achievement. How can one accomplish this - or do even better?

As in the stock market, the name of the game is information. Within broad limits, the betting market is likely to be efficient in this sense. But the returns on different horses need not be equal if people who bet at the track are at all sensitive to the differential risk involved in betting on one horse rather than another.

In discussing the stock market, we argued that holders of riskier stocks must earn a higher rate of return on the average than holders of less risky stocks. If they did not receive this higher return, risk-averse investors simply would not hold the riskier stocks. In racetrack betting, however, we seem to be dealing with risk lovers, people whose utility or satisfaction actually diminishes when risk is lower. In this circumstance, the returns on less risky horses must be higher, or less negative, on average; otherwise, no one would bet on these horses. This may seem counterintuitive, but it is a direct consequence of the fact that horse race bettors love risk.

In an environment in which risk matters to people, it should be no surprise that some horses exhibit higher average returns than others. The question of efficiency then comes down to this: Can above-average returns be earned by betting "scientifically," once the risk of various horses is accounted for? The answer is an unequivocal "yes."

REFUTING RACE TRACK MYTHS

Before developing the rules, procedures, and techniques of professionalism, we should destroy some of the persistent fallacies and misconceptions that have attached themselves to racing like barnacles to a boat. These misconceptions range from the nature of the bettor himself to the nature of the game itself.

<u>Misconception</u>: Betting on horses is just for compulsive losers. Forget the cliché of the racetrack hanger-on, the touts, drifters, and con men from the pages of Damon Runyon; men with colorful names, wide ties, and loud, checked sports jackets. They are gamblers in the worst sense. They talk big, look for easy marks, bet hunches and inside information, and always wind up losing.

Today's successful racetrack investor is more likely to be a retired military man, an accountant, or an ambitious junior executive seeking to augment his income. He is no gambler. He considers himself a speculative investor, handles himself accordingly. He has mastered a skill. He can control both his nerves and his greed; he is in it for the money alone. Any man can make race betting a successful business if he has the self-control and discipline to do it.

Some people do gamble for the sake of gambling; to them the action is everything and the thrill of the game is paramount. Gambling is then a sickness. Long years of experience have convinced me that the track is a great place for a man to discover himself. If he does not know himself, a little time spent betting sizable amounts of money will bring him face to face with sad reality. The track can be a natural home for the born loser, a haven for the superstitious, and a nightmare for the weak and timid. But it doesn't have to be.

Misconception: You can beat a race but you cannot beat the races. Nonsense! Contrary to what the losers say (and they are in the majority), you can beat the races. Hundreds do so, systematically, carefully, thoughtfully, unemotionally, almost scientifically. With intelligence, patience, and self-control, they have either a lucrative avocation or a very profitable profession. Actually, the old saying is backward. I believe you cannot beat a given race with any degree of certainty, considering all the variables involved. There are too many ways to lose a single race. But by playing the percentages, you can beat the races.

You might say we are operating with "actuarial" tables, just as the insurance companies do, to produce a large percentage of winners. An insurance company knows that a certain number of its policyholders are going to die in a certain period of time. It does not know which ones, but it is certain how many. In the

27

same way, we cannot know which of our standout horses will win. We know, however, that we will have the best horse often enough to produce a profit.

The "Dr. Weiss" method will set rules, which, if followed, will assure you consistent winnings month after month. Viewed strictly as a business, it has no inventory, no employees or office rent, and no stoppages or layoffs.

One thing that must be stressed: this book is not for the gambler, the stabber, the plunger, or the hunch player. It is for those who want to make it a business. No professional was ever successful without exacting preparation. No lawyer would enter court without detailed briefs. No businessman would go to a board meeting without all his facts and figures, anymore than a doctor would attempt an operation without being aware of all the latest techniques.

Misconception: Horseplayers all die broke. Don't believe it! Gamblers die broke, horseplayers only die bald. Don't gamble. Your approach is always that of a speculative investor. I can truthfully say that there is more larceny and carefully developed mendacity per square inch on the floor of the New York Stock Exchange and the Chicago Board of Trade than there is at any racetrack in the country. Also, you will find more pertinent information in the *Racing Form* applying to handicapping the horses than you can find in the *Wall Street Journal* concerning stocks, bonds, and commodities.

Horse racing has a bad reputation in some circles but any industry that handles as much money as racing does will always attract some people with bad reputations, and larcenous intentions. Some people, to be sure, attempt to fix races, and jockeys have been known to pull horses. Some of these efforts are successful. Yet, there are many more killings in the corporate world with spin-offs, stock options, and mergers than ever occur at a racetrack. You can operate safely on the assumption that horse racing is basically honest and carefully controlled. You can assume that racing gives you a fair run for your money. The people in the industry have too much at stake to allow it to do anything else.

Misconception: Gambling is somehow immoral. Discard this idea, too. Like all generalizations, it ignores important specific differences. First, why do most people gamble? Probably, because of the challenge. Certainly a feeling of power and exhilaration comes from beating the track. Most of us remember the daring and importance we felt in our imaginations as kids. At the gambling table we can continue such fantasies, rebelling against the conformity society imposes on us. At the gambling table a man is really on his own, alone against the world, defying for a moment all the conventions of society, church, and family. There is nothing wrong with getting a kick out of gambling, unless that is the primary focus.

To the true gambler, however, gambling is a form of escapism, perhaps a kind of psychological masochism. At the track or the table, the gambler can take a beating, he can fail, but he can blame the fates for his bad luck.

Losing also serves as an excuse to go back and get beaten again. The true gambler plays for the excitement of the game itself and, while not admitting it, probably wants to lose since it reinforces his contention that he is alone against the cruel and unyielding world. For this man gambling is a disease, one very difficult to cure.

In summary, betting on the horses is a gamble only if you make it a gamble. The subject of professionalism and professional behavior at the track will be covered in great detail later. For the moment, remember that betting is a demanding business. You must tie your hands with so many rules that you are not allowed to go plunging recklessly or betting wildly. Be a professional.

Misconception: You cannot make money at the track because of the overhead. The track and the State take too large a cut. The argument goes that after the track and the State take their 16 percent off the top, both agencies also keep what is called breakage, the odd pennies and nickels. For example, the winner that should really pay $6.85 actually pays just $6.80. The pay is always rounded off to the nearest dime and the bettor is always the loser, so the total skim-off Is closer to 17 percent, a little more in some states, a little less in others. Consequently, it you pick a horse that should pay $10.00, what you get back is $8.40. So the pari-mutuel system is the reason you cannot win at the races.

Do not believe it. The take does exist, but if you are getting $6.00 on a horse that ought to be even money and has a 1-1 chance of winning you have an overlay and thus a good bet. You can eliminate all thoughts of the track cut, the breakage, the take for the State, as well as the take for the horsemen and the race purses. This is your cost of doing business, the payment you make for the protection of the thoroughbred racing boards that control the business.

The take doesn't prevent you from being a long-term winner at the track. Only your lack of self-control will do that.

Again, this brings up the inescapable human element. It is a lonely business and many things can happen to shake your self-confidence. This cannot be stressed too much. Unless you have self-control, self-confidence, and can withstand the bad days, you cannot make it. If you have no self-control, your chance of ever being among those five percent who beat the races is less than nothing. What you must do to be successful is to be absolutely, coldly, brutally logical. A good businessman knows he has to make his decisions on the basis of logic and common sense if he is going to succeed. You have to do the same thing at the track. You are going to learn how to accomplish that. If properly handled, the rules set down in this book will make for profitable selections. In a matter of a few hours you are going to be better than 95 percent of the people who bet the horses. Again, you have to have an organized approach and the courage to stay with it. Always remember, the ability to pass a race is a tremendous advantage to you. Practice it.

Look at the mathematics of betting the favorites: 30 to 33 percent winners. Say that in the next 100 races we get 33 winners. A $2.00 flat bet in those 100 races will cost $200. What is the average return on those 33 winners that we had? Our figures show that the last 2,000 races at Hollywood Park, Santa Anita, and Del Mar, the favorites averaged $5.20 return. Therefore, those 33 winners paying $5.20 each returned $171.60 and we have bet $200. As a result we show a loss of $28.40. By eliminating a few false favorites, and betting more on outstanding selections we can turn a profit. How easily? Simply by increasing the win percentage to 40%. That's 7 more winners in 100 races! As you will see, that's easy to do!

There are only three different kinds of bettors who hold erroneous attitudes toward betting favorites. The first group plays only the favorites and plays any favorite at any odds. The second group looks at short-priced favorites with a jaundiced eye and avoids them because they are favorites. They pass up excellent horses who are tempting overlays because someone once told them not to bet on favorites. The third group believed that the longer-priced horses are more profitable but, without any real knowledge of handicapping, pick a horse only because he has high odds rather than because he has a good chance of winning. All three systems result in disaster.

You should pick your horse the night before the race, using an organized, systematic procedure. You probably agree by now that the approach explained in this book is going to be somewhat unorthodox in terms of usually accepted procedures. This approach, which I call the "Dr. Weiss" method, is different and you will do things in a different way, one that is successful. Other sacred cows around the track will be attacked and discredited throughout the book.

You have probably noticed how many times the phrases 'business" and "business principles" have been used. That is no accident. You must assume this approach if you are to succeed. This is an entirely new and unique approach to the business of making money betting on horses. It combines, compiles, and organizes many of the known and essential facts about racing, formulates them into rules, then teaches you the rules that offer positive result. You must understand and use the rules to profit by them. If you follow them, they will prevent mistakes.

Everything is organized, including how to bet, when to bet, and how much to bet. Nothing is left to chance or vagaries of hunches. You can honestly make as much money as you want to. The rules are simple, understandable, and sensible. You cannot keep from making the right decision.

Very little benefit will come to you from all this if you are, by nature, a gambler. You are not being encouraged to gamble. As a matter of fact you are urged to give it up and operate on a sound, professional basis. There is no magic formula for success . . . only knowledge. And knowledge is truly powerful.

BETTING ODDS

As we have said, betting odds are, in effect, the prices of the horses running in a race. The odds tell you how much you will be paid if you bet on a particular horse to win a race and that horse does win. For example, say the odds on Fast Runner are 8 to 1 (usually shown simply as "3" on the racetrack displays, known as "tote boards"). This means that every dollar you bet on Fast Runner will win you $3 (in addition to the $1 you bet in the first place) if he wins the race. A $2 bet on a first-place winning horse will give you a payoff of $8: the $6 return indicated by the 3 to 1 odds, plus your initial $2 "investment." Table 1-1 shows the approximate payoffs to bets of various sizes at various odds. Just one word of caution at this point. The racetrack offers a wide variety of bets, which we are about to describe. But the odds are usually displayed for only one type: win bets. If you engage in other types of wagering, your prospective payoff will not always be so clear - in fact, it will at limes prove quite difficult to estimate.

Odds	$2 Payoff	Odds	$2 Payoff	Odds	$2 Payoff
1/9	$2.20	8/5	$5.20	7/1	$16.00
1/5	$2.40	9/5	$5.60	8/1	$18.00
2/5	$2.80	2/1	$6.00	9/1	$20.00
1/2	$3.00	5/2	$7.00	10/1	$22.00
3/5	$3.20	3/1	$8.00	11/1	$24.00
4/5	$3.60	7/2	$9.00	12/1	$26.00
1/1	$4.00	4/1	$10.00	13/1	$28.00
6/5	$4.40	9/2	$11.00	14/1	$30.00
7/5	$4.80	5/1	$12.00	15/1	$32.00
3/2	$5.00	6/1	$14.00	16/1	$34.00

TYPES OF BETS

Betting on a race is an easy thing to do. You simply go on-line and click on the selected track, race number, horse number, and amount.

Win-Place-Show Bets. These are the oldest, and undoubtedly the best-known, racetrack bets. A win bet is just what it sounds like. You bet that a particular horse will win a particular race; if it does, you receive a payoff; if not, you get nothing. Actually, that is not precisely true: You still have your ticket (which you would have to present for the payoff, had your horse won), and these make excellent bookmarks.

A place bet pays off if your horse finishes first or second; otherwise it does not pay off. Whether the horse is first or second does not affect the size of your payoff. The good news about this type of bet is obvious: It pays off more frequently than does a win bet (this is because your horse-indeed, any horse-has a better chance of finishing first or second than of finishing first!). The bad news is that the payoffs to place bets tend to be lower. The reason is again obvious: The sum total bet on all horses to place (called the place pool) must be shared by backers of the first two finishers, not merely the backers of the first horse. The more people you share with, the less you yourself receive.

Note, however, that your contingent payoff on a place bet-the amount you will collect if your horse runs first or second - cannot be precisely inferred from the odds on your horse. There are two reasons why not. First, the payoffs to place bets depend solely on patterns of betting in the place pool. These patterns may or may not approximate closely the odds on win bets, which is what the track displays on its "tote boards." The second reason why the place payoff is unpredictable is that it depends on the amounts bet both on your horse and on the other top finisher. It therefore matters which horse "comes in" with yours; but this is something that cannot be known until the race is over. How the place pool is divided among bettors on the first two horses is clearly a matter of interest and importance. Suffice it to say for the moment that you are best off sharing the pool with as few others as possible.

A show bet is similar to a place bet, but it covers the first three finishers. You get a payoff if your horse comes in first, second, or third; otherwise you get nothing. The order of finish within the top three doesn't affect the payoff. As a rule, you will collect more frequent payoffs betting to show than to win or place, but not surprisingly, they will usually be smaller. There is also somewhat more uncertainty about the size of these payoffs: Racetracks do not display show odds, and your prospective payoff now depends on two other finishers whose identity is unknown   until the race is over.

You will sometimes hear references to combination or across-the-board bets. These refer to a bet on a particular one to win, place, and show, with equal sums on each possibility. Thus, a "$6 combination on number seven" is a bet of $2 to win, $2 to place, and $2 to show on horse number seven. The payoffs in a race are typically reported in the following form:

Horse	Win	Place	Show
Dr. Fager	8.80	5.20	3.60
Damascus		4.20	3.20
Bold Hour			5.80

Let's translate. Dr. Fager won this race and paid $8.80 for a $2 win ticket. Payoffs are always stated in terms of a $2 bet, the minimum that the tracks permit. A $2 place ticket on Dr. Fager would retrieve $5.20, and a show ticket, $3.60 (it is not logically impossible for a horse to pay more to show than to place, or more to place than to win, since each payoff depends on the pattern of betting in a completely separate pool. You will observe the first of these events occasionally, but the second is exceedingly rare. Damascus, the second-place finisher, paid $9.20 to place and $5.00 to show; and the number three finisher, Bold Hour, paid $2.80 to show. Notice, as we pointed out, that the order of finish does not determine the size of the payoff within the top group; the payoffs depend solely on how much money has been bet on each of the horses in the pertinent betting pool.

Exotic Bets. These refer to a variety of "compound" bets on two or more horses. The exotics are low-probability wagers. And you will have to overcome a "take" as high as 30. The most common, not all of which are offered at all tracks, include the following:

Exacta (sometimes called "perfecta"). You select the number one and number two finishers in a given race, specifying the order. If your horses finish 1-2 in the specified order, you win; otherwise you lose. Should the animals you pick 1-2 finish 2-1, that's a loser and a heartbreaker; exacta players frequently bet a pair both ways. They are also prone to "wheel" a horse. Wheeling means that you couple your horse in a series of exacta bets with all other entrants - if, for example, you are convinced that Damascus is going to run away from the field in today's race, you buy exacta tickets that pick Damascus number one, and each rival horse number two on one of your tickets. Wheels obviously can become quite expensive, especially if you wheel "both ways"-in our example, adding to the tickets above a second set in which Damascus is picked to run second, and each rival is picked first in turn.

Quinella. You select the first two finishers in a race. The bet is won if the horses you pick are the first two, regardless of the order. Any other result and you lose your bet.

Trifecta. This is like the exacta, but you select the first three finishers in order. You win if, and only if, the horses you pick 1-2-3 come in 1-2-3. You may of course wheel here as well, but this can run into truly big money. Quite obviously, the trifecta is a low probability (or long-odds) bet in most instances, and the payoffs, accordingly, can be extremely large.

Daily Double. This is a bet in which you pick the winners of two consecutive races. You win your bet if both picks come in first; otherwise you lose. The daily double is very similar to what is known as a parlay - that is, betting on a horse in the first race, and, if you win, betting your entire payoff on a horse in the next race. Traditionally, the tracks offer daily double bets on the first two races of the day. This type of betting is now so popular, however, that you may also be offered a "late double" involving two consecutive races toward the end of the day.

Big Q. This is, in effect, a parlay of two quinellas in consecutive races. You pick the first two finishers, regardless of order, in the first race; if you win, your winning ticket entitles you to a similar choice (rather than a cash payoff) in the second race.

Pick Four (or Pick Six, etc.). These bets (sometimes called Super Four, etc.) are structurally like the daily double except that you must pick winners in four (or six) consecutive races. Your chances of winning such bets are slim, but the payoff if you do hit it is likely to be high.

You will encounter other kinds of exotic betting at some racetracks, but all are variations on the same theme. In each instance, you must pick two or more horses to finish in specified positions (with some flexibility only in the quinella). In an actuarial sense, the exotics are poorer bets than "straight" win, place, or show; this is because most states allow the tracks to take a larger share out of exotic betting pools, thereby lowering the expected dollar value of your bets. But if you like to gamble on improbable, but big, prizes-as many people do-this is where the action is. Beware, however. Numerous agonies are likely to accompany your occasional jackpots.

The morning line odds (or simply the morning line) are shown for each horse in the "graded entries" of the Daily racing Form. These are the "starting" odds that you and other track patrons see before the betting on a race begins. The morning line represents the best guess of the track's expert (sometimes called a "handicapper") about the horses' relative chances of winning. The morning line on a horse that is, 8 to 1. The expert is stating that this animal has only a one in nine chance to win the race.

A couple of salient points about the morning line odds are worth bearing in mind. First, these odds simply represent the racetrack handicapper's best guess about the winning probabilities of the entrants. As we shall see below, these estimates do contain real informa-tion, as we will see shortly. One cannot make money using these data alone. Second, once the betting begins, it is the pattern of the bets that determines the actual odds. The payoffs to winning bets are determined by the final odds, when the betting ends and the race begins. (Typically, the betting period lasts 20 to 25 minutes.)

Consider an example. Let's suppose that a horse who is 8 to 1 in the morning line. Few track patrons believe that he has a real chance to win, and by the time the betting ends, his odds are 22 to 1. This means, in effect, that the "market's" opinion of the horse is a good deal worse than that of the track handicapper. It also means that if you bet $2 on such a horse to win, and he does win, your payoff will be quite healthy - roughly $46 (the $44 suggested by the 22 to 1 odds plus the refund of your original $2 investment). We say "roughly" because the reported odds are rounded; the true odds are unlikely to be exactly 22.000 to 1.

This aspect of odds and betting is worth dwelling on for a moment. What we observe at the racetrack is something quite unlike a bet in roulette, blackjack, or craps. In those games the "odds" and payoffs are fixed (at different levels for different types of bets). If you put down $5 on number 17 in roulette and number 17 comes up, your payoff is the same ($180), regardless of how much money others have (or have not) bet on that number. In contrast, the payoff to a winning bet on a horse is determined by the proportion of the handle that is bet on that horse (the handle is the sum total of bets on all entrants). This is what is frequently referred to as a pari-mutuel betting system: The payoffs are determined (or "driven") by the pattern of the bets.

THE NECESSARY INGREDIENTS TO WIN

There are, in fact, two aspects necessary to win at the racetrack. 1) Choosing the right horse. 2) Money management. Almost every book written on racetrack wagering focuses solely on choosing the right horse. But that's only half the story. The other half you're obviously supposed to find out on your own.

This book will provide you with a proven system of choosing and betting horses. It has worked for two decades.

It is not necessary to "know" horses. In fact, having previous "handicapping" skills can be a distinct disadvantage. This isn't a treatise about how to "read" the Racing Form. This is about using statistics to overcome the odds. Over the course of a meet certain stats always hold true…time after time, year after year.

A great piece of advice came from the late Walter Haight, the racing columnist of The Washington Post, who said," A horseplayer should maintain a betting fund completely separate from the money he lives on." This is especially important if one is married, so that cycles at the races track do not interfere with the ability to pay bills for rent, food, etc.

One of the benefits of a system is that it takes emotions out of play. Most handicappers are influenced by a myriad of factors. These outside influences often lead to emotional, not logical actions. It is essential to follow the system

There is tendency to circumvent the system when one is winning consistently. It is called "The Messiah Complex." You feel that everything you pick comes in. However, this system is designed to eliminate such possibilities.

HANDICAPPING BY THE DR. WEISS METHOD

We are now ready to enter the handicapping phase. From now on we are going to be looking at actual races, analyzing point by point the conditions of each race. We are going to apply 23 criteria to each race. The horse that qualifies will be our bet.

Study the figures in Table I. They are the result of three decades of analysis of thousands of races.

The Winning Statistics (Table 1) and accompanying 23 rules are the heart and soul of the "Dr. Weiss" handicapping method. Study these criteria; know then thoroughly. Believe me, they are your key to riches. These statistics were painstakingly gathered over a three-decade period at the major tracks, and they will hold true for any major track in the country.

TABLE I: WINNING STATISTICS (based on 7,000+ races)

Recency And Condition:

63.2% of winner Ran last race within 10 days

84.3% of winner ran last race within 30 days

15.7% of winnersran last race over 30 days ago

Weight

47.2% of winner carried same weight as in last race

31.1% of winner carried less weight than in last race

20.8% of winner carried more weight than in last race

Class

90.7% of winner ran In same class as last race or lower

9.3% of winner ran in higher class than last race

Finish in Last Race

58.5% of winners finished first, second or third

60.3% of winners finished within 2 lengths and gained in the stretch run

50

Speed

80.0% of winners were among three highest speed ratings

Age

76.9% of winners were four-year-olds and older

23.1% of winners were three-year-olds

Distance

51.6% of winner ran same distance as last race

27.3% of winners ran longer distance than last race

21.0% of winners ran shorter distance than last race

Sex

75.6% of races were won by males, colts, geldings

24.3% were won by females

Odds

84.1% of winners were among three favorites

We want the averages, the percentages, to be on our side when we make a bet. This is the only way to succeed.

Three of these statistical sets will lead to a definite rule to guide you in your selections. To make absolutely sure you understand them and their significance, examine then in order.

1. Recency and Condition

Study these figures. Herein lies the key to your success. What do these figures tell you? In 7,000 races at the major race tracks an analysis of the winners of those races showed only 785 or 15.7 percent were able to win a race after a layoff of longer than 30 days. That means if you are going to be betting on a selection that has not run within 30 days of today's race, you are leaving yourself wide open to disaster. You are taking the absolute worst of it in terms of the percentages. Yet the group of horses that ran within the past 30 days will produce the winner 84.3 percent of the time! Therefore, if you limit your activities to those horses that ran recently you have a much better chance of selecting a live horse that can win the race. Check the date of the horse's last race. He/she must have run within 30 days. Do not bet on a horse that has not run within 30 days. I give a two-day leeway to stakes horses and horses than have a four point or higher Byer speed rating advantage per race.

2. Weight

Our second step is to eliminate from consideration any horse that is carrying more weight than he carried the last time, or more than he carried in a winning effort (or a race in which he finished in the same class or within two lengths of the winner with the same weight within 90 days). The old adage "weight can stop a train" is true. The horse that has an increased load to carry today is at a distinct disadvantage against equal contenders who have weight off.

The winning statistics show that 78.3 percent of all the horses able to win races did so carrying the same weight or less weight than in their last race. Only 20 percent were able to do so carrying more weight, even an additional pound. We will not be quite that stringent with our rules. We will accept a horse going up a pound or two if he shows us he has carried that much weight in the past 90 days. Eliminate any horse carrying more weight than he carried last time, or more than he carried in the average of his last five races, a key point that your competitors at the track often overlook.

3. Class

Astounding figures! Again, your competitors out at the track, with only a few exceptions, do not know this. Everybody has the general idea that class is important and that a high-class horse will beat a low-class horse. We want you to analyze these figures, however, to realize the tremendous significance of class. In the 5,000 races analyzed, only 9 percent of them were won by a horse that was able to go up in class, even a little, over his previous race. We will not be quite that stringent. We might consider a horse going up in class provided he has run a good race (within 2 lengths of the winner) at a higher class level recently (90 days)

A genuine advantage in class by a horse can outweigh just about any other factor or combination of factors. Class definitely must be given the highest priority. Eliminate any horse that is going up in class. In an allowance race he must have been running against allowance horses. In a stakes race or handicap race, he must have been running in stakes or handicap races. Do not, however, be misled that class is the only factor and do not automatically decide to bet on the horse with the highest class. It does not work that way. All the factors have to be taken into consideration. The high-class horse will not win if he is not ready, if he is not in shape and is not carrying the proper weight.

To be considered an allowance horse he must do more than just compete against allowance horses. He must give some sign of being able to hold his own. If a horse has a poor performances at a certain level, it is almost impossible to pinpoint his real class. It is only when he begins to run good races and hold his own against present company that an inkling emerges as to his real class.

If the horse turns in a strong effort (see rule #4), it is an excellent candidate for a repeat win if he is in his element and comes back within thirty days.

A horse's chances are increased if he drops in class, under normal conditions.

Now that you have eliminated all the horses that cannot qualify under the first three rules you are ready to apply the final equalizer.

4. Finish in last race

A horse may figure head and shoulders above its competition in a given race, based on speed, class, and weight. However, if he is not in condition to use that speed and class today, he will not win today! He may have definite superiority in speed . . . and be beaten by a slower horse today. Our most reliable tool in determining the ability of the horse to run today is a careful inspection of his recent races.

5. Speed

It is a fact that 80 percent of all winners in the 7,000 races analyzed were found in a group with the three highest speed ratings. Yet we cannot judge a horse solely by his rating. Speed becomes a factor, because now we are dealing with horses that have indicated they are ready to live up to their speed potential today.

6-. Age

Clearly three-year-olds running against older horses have a serious disadvantage. They are, with few exceptions, not as mature and strong as the older horses. Our system avoids three-year-olds against older horses.

7. Distance

These figures lead us to no specific rule, since they do not show a noticeable disparity. Our winners do, however, establish a pattern. Apparently a fit and well meant horse can stretch out to a longer distance. It seems a bit more difficult for the established router to accept a shorter distance. By the time he gets into full stride, the speedsters have built up such a commanding lead they can often coast home.

The obvious move is to prefer those horses that are running at the same distance as their last race. This would add strength to any signal from the previous race. Other factors being equal, it is wiser to choose the horse coming back today at the same distance.

8. Sex

Alas for equal rights, the figures don't lie. Weight concessions and all, the girls simply cannot beat boys of equal age and experience. In the shorter races they sometimes (rarely) can hold their speed and hold off the sturdier males. At distances the prospect becomes more and more remote. They can be selected only on those rare occasions when they can boast an extreme superiority in most departments. Almost always you must prefer the males.

9. Odds

Limit your handicapping to those three horses that are the lowest odds as posted by the morning line. Limit your analysis to these three favorites and you will be dealing with the winner 84 percent of the time! Only 16 percent of the 7,000 races were won by what may be called an "outsider."

FAVORITES VS. LONG SHOTS – THE BETTER INVESTMENT

In this chapter we begin a detailed examination of the empirical evidence on the profitability of betting on horses. The first question we ask is how to measure the betting public's subjective assessment of each horse's winning chances. It is clear that this is

appropriately measured by the proportion of the entire betting pool that is bet on the individual horses. If the public (in the aggregate) thinks that a given horse has four out of ten chances of winning a given race, it will bet 40 percent of all the moneys bet in that race on the given horse. We call this proportion the subjective probability of winning, and it is closely related to the odds on the horse in question.

The public may or may not be right in its assessment. Horses that have 40 percent of all moneys bet on them may win more than 40 percent of the time or less than 40 percent of the time. We can calculate this objective winning probability by taking the historical record of all horses that have had 40 percent of the betting pool bet on them and simply counting the percentage of races they have actually won.

If the public's assessment of horses' winning chances were perfect, the subjective and objective probabilities would be the same. In fact, they tend to be close, but with one persistent quirk: Favorites (horses with high winning chances) have higher objective probabilities than subjective probabilities, with the reverse being true for long shots. This means, that if the public makes the favorite 2:1, its chances of winning a race are better than two to one. This discrepancy increases as favorites go lower in odds. We describe this empirical regularity by saying that favorites are underbet and long shots are overbet. The reasons for this phenomenon are open to speculation, but the profound consequence is that you will make out better on the average by betting on favorites.

Is this kind of situation compatible with the assumption that bettors as a group are thoroughly informed about each horse's ability and winning chances and are out to maximize their gain? Clearly not. Everybody is just as able as we are (and as many other researchers who have found the same results) to determine the greater profitability of betting on favorites; if people acted in their own self-interest, they would increase the amounts bet on favorites relative to long shots. This would lower the payoffs on favorites relative to long shots, until on balance no differentials would exist among homes in different odds categories. We describe the actual situation by saying that the betting market is not efficient, since it does not use all useful information that is potentially available.

THE SUBJECTIVE AND OBJECTIVE
PROBABILITIES OF WINNING

If the objective probability were 0.3, this would mean that if this horse ran a very large number of comparable races, it would win very close to 30 percent of them. The measurement of subjective probabilities is easy. All we have to do is to divide the amount bet on a horse by the total win pool. It is obviously very difficult to measure a single horse's objective probability of winning. The best we can probably do without an enormous amount of effort is to consider groups of comparable horses and see what fraction of them actually won.

The next obvious question is how we should find groups of comparable horses. One way is to assume that horses with the same or very similar odds tend to be comparable. What we therefore do is to group horses by their odds. We take a set of many races and put the horse with the lowest odds in each race into Group 1, the horse with the second lowest odds in each race in Group 2, and so on. Each horse in Group 1 has its own particular odds, and they are all slightly different, ranging perhaps from 1 to 2 to, say, 3 to 2. In Group 2, the odds might range from 1 to 5 to 2, and so on. Then, within each group, we can average these subjective probabilities together. This is the procedure for estimating the subjective winning probability of the horses in each group.

Now, how do we get an estimate of the objective probability of winning in each group? The simplest way is to let the record speak for itself! We shall just count how many horses in each group actually won, as a percentage of the total number of horses in that group. Table 6-1 illustrates this comparison for 729 races in Atlantic City, N.J. in 1978, including a total of 5,805 horses. The objective probability equate to the percentage of horses that actually won. The subjective probability equates to the betting odds.

Table 6-1   Objective and Subjective Probabilities

Groups	Number of Horses in Group	Objectiv Probabil
Favorites	729	.361
Second-lowest odds	729	.218
Third-lowest odds	729	.170
Fourth-lowest odds	724	.115
Fifth-lowest odds	692	.071
Sixth-lowest odds	598	.050
Seventh-lowest odds	431	.030
Eighth-lowest odds	289	.017
Ninth-lowest odds	165	.006

First, note that the groups in Table 6-1 are based on different numbers of horses; this is obvious when you consider that some races have only six or seven horses running, and in such races there cannot be a home with "eighth-lowest odds" or "ninth-lowest odds." Second, it is interesting to observe that the subjective and objective probabilities are apparently quite close. The third and most interesting thing to note is that for horses with low odds (favorites and near-favorites), the objective probability of winning is quite a bit higher than the subjective probability, whereas for long shots (in our table, horses with seventh-, eighth-, and ninth-lowest odds), the exact reverse is true. What this says is that the betting public consistently <u>overestimates</u> the winning chances of <u>long shots</u> (horses with low objective probabilities of winning) and consistently <u>underestimates</u> the winning chances of <u>favorites</u>.

This is perhaps the most fundamental and well-confirmed empirical regularity in racetrack betting. For example, Table 6-2 (based on 10,000 races) in which the groups are explicitly identified as ranges of odds. Exactly the same phenomenon is observable in Table 6-2 as in Table 6-1: Favorites or near-favorites are "underbet" and long shots are "overbet." We say that favorites are "underbet" because if more had been bet on them, the subjective probability computed for these horses would have risen to be more nearly equal to the objective probability (which, of course, remains unaffected by how much people bet.

Table 6-2   Fabricand's Data

Odds	Number of Horses Entered	Objective Probability	Subjec Probab
0.40-0.55	129	0.713	0.56
0.60-0.75	295	0.553	0.50
0.80-0.95	470	0.513	0.44
1.00-1.15	615	0.470	0.40
1.20-1.35	789	0.403	0.37
1.40-1.55	874	0.379	0.34
1.60-1.75	954	0.355	0.31
1.80-1.95	1,051	0.309	0.29
2.00-2.45	3,223	0.289	0.26
2.50-2.95	3,623	0.230	0.22
3.00-3.45	3,807	0.209	0.20
3.50-3.95	3,652	0.186	0.18
4.00-4.45	3,296	0.161	0.16
4.50-4.95	3,129	0.155	0.14
5.00-5.95	5,586	0.123	0.13
6.00-6.95	5,154	0.110	0.11
7.00-7.95	4,665	0.099	0.10
8.00-8.95	3,990	0.082	0.09
9.00-9.95	3,617	0.082	0.08
10.00-14.95	12,007	0.060	0.06
15.00-19.95	7,041	0.040	0.04
20.00-99.95	25,044	0.014	0.02

A major unresolved question is why this type of discrepancy is observed over and over again. It is practically an empirical "law" in racetrack betting, and many academic studies have speculated on the possible reasons for it. We shall briefly examine the principal theories.

The first and perhaps oldest theory is that the betting public has a special taste, a "yen," for betting on long shots, at the same time that it has a special distaste for betting on favorites.

Betting on favorites may be perceived as a stodgy thing to do, while betting on long shots has a certain zip to it; moreover, if you win, you can tell all your friends about it and gain admiration! If this is true, we would expect to see pretty much what we do observe.

RATES OF RETURN

If we are to compare the profitability of racetrack betting with any other kind of investment activity, we must define the rate of return from each of these activities. This may not be so easy for an investment that has a "lifetime" of many years and provides the owner an income stream over such a long period. Since a rate of return calculation for such an investment involves the comparison of present-day dollars with future dollars, it must make use of the interest rate which is the rate at which future and present dollars can be transformed into each other.

Fortunately, our racetrack case is simpler because we usually want to compare the rate of return from investing in one horse to that of another horse in the same race. Betting on a horse is an "investment," with at most 20 minutes duration.

We calculated the rates of return for the sample of horses discussed in Table 6-1, but now we have aggregated the horses into groups a little differently, by odds-levels, and a little more coarsely than in Table 6-2. We did this twice: once for all the races and once only for the late races (i.e., the eighth and ninth races of each racing day). Our purpose was to see if rates of return in late races differ from their average in all races. The results are continued in Table 6-3.

Note that all rates of return are negative; hence, on the average, bettors lose no matter what odds horse they bet on. Interestingly, the loss is only - 13.7 percent if you bet on horses with odds less than 2, which is quite a bit less than the 17 to 18 percent loss that bettors in the aggregate must lose because of the track's take. Looking down the middle column of the table, we see that the returns fluctuate in no particularly orderly manner, but it is noteworthy that long shots - that is, horses with odds higher than 25 - make a whopping 64 percent loss on every dollar bet!

Table 6-3   Rates of Return from Asch-Malkiel-Qua

Odds Level D	Average Rate of Return in All Races
$D \leq 2$	-.137
$2 < D \leq 3.5$	-.318
$3.5 < D \leq 5$	-.176
$5 < D \leq 8$	-.224
$8 < D \leq 14$	-.160
$14 < D \leq 25$	-.326
$25 < D$	-.637

This certainly confirms what we discussed in the previous section: Long shots are overbet - that is, their odds and payoffs are lower than is justified by their objective chances of winning (and the converse is true for favorites). This tendency, if anything, is all the more apparent for the late races. Here, betting on the short-odds horses is almost a fair (break-even) game, and the loss on the long shots is greater still.

Why should the late races be any different from the earlier ones? This fact is based on the following. When one goes to the track, the normal expectation is that he will lose money. By the time the seventh race is over, one has lost $50, and he is worried that when he gets home his wife will apply a rolling pin to his backside. He must, at all costs, recoup. Betting on favorites will hardly make him recoup because their payoffs are so low; even though he would be relatively likely to win, he would diminish his losses from $50 to, say, only $40 or $80, and that is not enough to avert the dreaded specter of the rolling pin

He must bet on long shots to have any chance of winning or even breaking even. So long shots are over bet in late races even more than in the early ones.

Look now at the far right column of Table 6-2. These are the average rates of return for that particular sample, and they tell a very similar story to that of Table 6-3; the only exception is that the rate of return to horses with odds less than 0.55 is actually positive! This seems to suggest that betting on such horses - very heavy favorites - will actually make money in the long run. Note, however, that one would have to do a lot of waiting to take advantage of this, since most races do not have horses with odds that low. In fact, only 129 out of the 93,011 horses analyzed had odds less than 0.55 (roughly 1 to 2).

In table 6-4, simply put, we see that the lower a horses' odds, the greater the chances of wining. Conversely, the higher a horse's odds the less the chance of winning. But even more important, the chances of a horse winning or losing grows proportionality larger as we move to the extremes.

Table 6-4   Expected Values and Variances

Odds	Expected Values
0.40– 0.55	0.028
0.60– 0.75	−0.097
0.80– 0.95	−0.063
1.00– 1.15	−0.051
1.20– 1.35	−0.109
1.40– 1.55	−0.089
1.60– 1.75	−0.076
1.80– 1.95	−0.135
2.00– 2.45	−0.099
2.50– 2.95	−0.173
3.00– 3.45	−0.147
3.50– 3.95	−0.153
4.00– 4.45	−0.185
4.50– 4.95	−0.141
5.00– 5.95	−0.236
6.00– 6.95	−0.209
7.00– 7.95	−0.188
8.00– 8.95	−0.253
9.00– 9.95	−0.170
10.00–14.95	−0.243
15.00–19.95	−0.302
20.00–99.95	−0.541

The conclusion that we have reached so far - tentatively and with qualifications – is that the betting market is not efficient. This means that all the information that exists about a race is not fully reflected in the odds; one can therefore be able to take profitable advantage of this.

HOW WELL DO ODDS PREDICT WINNERS?

We already know that horses with low odds have a relatively high probability of winning, and in this sense, the odds obviously are of some help in picking winners. The question we want to ask now is whether any refinements are possible that would allow us to do better. That is, can we coax more evidence out of the odds by eliminating "false favorites?

An interesting consequence of the logit prediction in this case is that the predicted winning probability for horse 1 is much higher than one would think from the morning line or the final odds. Whereas, for horse 3, which is by no means a slingshot, the reverse is true.

Table 6-6   Logit Predictions of Winning Probabilities for a Hypotheti·

Horse	Subjective Probability	Morning-Line-Odds-Based Probability	Final Odds
1	.30	.40	1.73
2	.25	.30	2.28
3	.20	.20	3.10
4	.15	.05	4.47
5	.07	.03	10.71
6	.03	.02	26.33

THE EIGHTEEN ESSENTIAL RULES OF
PICKING WINNERS

The rules for choosing a horse are simple. That is crucial. Systems only work when the rules are followed precisely. And only if the rules are clear and concise can that occur.

1). Only bet at Santa Anita, Hollywood Park, Del Mar, Aqueduct, Belmont, Arlington Park, Woodbine, Gulfstream Park, Hialeah Park, or Lone Star Park. These are the "A" tracks, where the best horses run. Higher quality horses run more consistently. Do not bet Saratoga. It is known as "the graveyard of favorites." Do not bet Keenland. The stretch is unusually long, which produces some very unexpected results.

2). Only bet allowance, or stake, or handicap races. The lesser the quality of horses, the more inconsistently they run.

3). Only bet races where there are 10 or fewer entrants. It is not enough to have the best horse; he or she must also get a "good trip." That is, not get blocked or forced to run wide. Something that occurs frequently with bigger fields.

4). Only bet a horse that is one of the three top picks by the morning line (also know as the graded entries). 84.1% of winners come from one of the top three consensus picks.

5). Only bet a horse that has one of the top three "Byer" speed ratings averaged for the past three races. 80% of winners had one of the top three speed ratings.

6). Bet to win only. There is a false sense of security betting place and show. The mathematics of betting is such that the tracks and the state extract a slightly higher percentage from the place and show pools. This adds up substantially in the long run. Win bets offer the best return over the long run – which is what we are concerning about.

7). Only bet a horse that has run within the past four weeks. 84.3% of winners ran within thirty days of their last race. Grant a three-day leeway for horses that have a three point or higher speed rating (per race) over the second choice. For stakes and handicap horses, the rule is 60 days.

8). Only bet a horse that is carrying the same or less weight than the last race. 78.3% of winners met this criterion. Unless the horse has shown the ability to carry today's weight at the same distance within the past 60 days.

9). Only bet a horse that finished first, second, or third in its last race, or has finished within 2 lengths of the winner in his last race. 60.3% of horses who won met this criteria.

10). Never bet a female against male horses. Males won 75.6% of mixed sex races.

11). Only bet a horse that is running in the same or longer distance than its last race. 78.6% of horses won under these conditions.

12). Only bet races 1 1/8th mile or less; longer races depend too much on pace, which can be dictated by and taken advantage of by lesser horses.

13). Never bet on an "off track." Bet only when the track conditions are fast. Just download the results of the first race at your track of choice. It will tell you the track condition that day. Rarely, if ever, will the first race provide a betting opportunity. The cheapest races are usually the early races.

14). Do not bet a horse going up in class. Do not bet a horse moving from a maiden race to an allowance race (unless all the rest of the horses are maidens). Do not bet an allowance horse moving up to a stakes race unless he or she has run in a stakes race in one of its previous three races. 90.7% of winners ran in the same or lesser class than their previous race.

15). Never bet grass races. Certain horses take to the surface, other don't. Also, the turns on the grass course are much tighter, making luck of the "trip" more of a factor.

16). Never bet a three year old against an older horse. 76% of such races were won by older horses. Unless the three year old has run against older horses in the same class and finished within 2 lengths of the winner in the past ninety days.

17). The top choice must have a Byer speed rating of at least 80, and be at least three points higher than the second rated horse (per race). If comparing for more than one race, use the three-point rule (six points higher for two races; nine points higher for three races). Never bet against the top speed rated horse. You are either betting on him because all the other factors confirm him, or you're not betting at all.

18). Do not bet at "cold" tracks (Woodbine, New York, Arlington in the winter).

All of this information is available to you in the Daily Racing Form. Now here is one of the miracles of the Internet. You can pick and choose which racetracks to bet, and further, which races to bet simply by going on line. The DRF has set up a beautiful, simple, highly accessible service. The first page tells you which tracks are currently open. Choose one of the approved tracks. Then look at the graded entries. See which races qualify. Down load the past performances for those races, then go to the next track and start with step one again. Within 10-15 minutes, you will have in front of you all of the races and entries needed for your analysis. You should be able to review each race in about 5-10 minutes.

BETTING BY THE DR. WEISS METHOD

Never bet with money you need for bills. Never bet money that is already committed to other obligations. Always keep some savings set aside for household emergencies. Don't use vacation money, or your Christmas fund. Only use a bankroll that is within your "comfort zone." If you lose it, it won't force you to move, change your life style, or severely impact your primary relationship. We will start with a hypothetical bankroll of $10,000. This will make he figures more simplistic and understandable. If you start with a different amount, the percentages will stay the same.

1)   Look up the morning line odds (the graded entries) for the horse chosen as a bet for that race. The morning line odds of the average bet found by the Dr. Weiss system is 1-1 (even money).

2)   Base bet - 12% of your capital on a horse that is **even** money. This percentage is based on mathematical algorithms, which maximize the amount bet and minimize the risk. Bet 12% of your bankroll on each selection. This way you will be betting more when you are ahead, and less when you are behind.

3)   For every up tick of the morning-line odds, bet ½ % less that 12%. E.g. If your selection has a

morning line odds of of 6-5, then bet ½ % less than the base bet of 12%, or 11.5%. If the horse is 4-5, then bet ½% more than 12%, or 12.5% of your capital.

4)   If your selection comes up in one of the last two races of the day, bet an additional ½ % of your capital after doing the above calculations. Favorites are underbet, long shots are over bet at the end of the day.

5)   If you start with $10,000 and you lose your first bet, then your betting capital will be plus or minus $8,800. Your next base bet will be $950 plus or minus the variables listed above.

THE BEST ADVICE

Never become a handicapper. It may make the process more interesting, but it is ultimately a losing proposition. Keep your views and beliefs out of the betting process. Allow the statistics to do the work for you. This method takes patience and requires consistency. Use a small hand-held calculator to determine the amount of each bet.

Don't try to make last minute calculations by hand. This system isn't glamorous, it just works. I do not end here wishing you good luck. Luck is for those unprepared and who allow their emotions to rule. You are not in that grouping. You will follow the rules and you will win. How much will be determined by your bankroll, access to a computer with high speed internet service, and having a half hour per day to analyze the many race cards available to you. See you in the "winner's circle."

APPENDIX "A" - INTERPRETING THE DAILY RACING FORM

Because of copy write laws, I cannot provide here samples of races from the Daily Racing Form. However, The Daily Racing From itself provides a wonderful, free tutorial. Take the time to study it carefully. Even if you have read the form before, there may be some facts you were not aware of. The past performances published by the *Daily Racing Form* will soon be your indispensable companion.

These incredibly accurate records give you all the Information necessary to select winners. The records published in the *Form* are actually digested and concentrated descriptions of a horse's performance in its most recent races. They give you a complete picture of the horse's performance and provide you with the data that lead to winners.

There is no other way of getting the necessary information. The results charts are helpful, but past performances from the *Racing Form* and the facts about the horse's prior races are absolutely essential. The past performance lines give you everything you need to know.

APPENDIX "B" SAMPLE RACES

Example #1

The sixth at Belmont, June 25, 2005. Precise Motion was coming back in 29 days, racing at the same distance, running in the same class, and dropping one pound. He finished 2 lengths behind the winner last time out. His speed rating is a phenomenal 12 points higher than the second best horse. Precise Motion was a 3 year old running against older horses, but he had just came off a race against older horses in the same class and finished second, two lengths behind the winner. Our system usually picks short price favorites. But in this case, Precise Motion paid $7.70!

Example #2

One of the most blatant examples of a false favorite occurred on June 11, 2005 at Hollywood Park. Fusiachi Samuria - the son of Fuchashi Pegasis (the horse that won the Kentucky Derby a few years back) – was running in a high-priced allowance race. Actually, it was more like a stakes race because a number of the horses had placed in some important stakes races. Fusciachi Samuri had won his first race – a maiden race – by two lengths in mediocre time, against maidens. He was coming back after a six month layoff, running against older horses, of a higher class, at a distance he had never run. He had basically every possible factor going against him. He went off at 3 to 5 and ran out of the money losing by more than 7 lengths.

Example Race #3

Here is an example of a four star bet. Dwango was running in the 8th at Belmont on July 2, 2005. Conditions were for three year olds and up; non-winners of two other than a maiden race. Dwango was four years old, running back in 21 days, carrying the same weight as last race, and dropping in class from alw 57,000 to alw 48,000. He was going up in distance, and finished within a ½ length of the winner in his last race. Best of all, his Byer speed rating was 13 points higher than the second pick! This was a classic. It doesn't get any better.

Example Race #4

And here's a classic false favorite. Winner was running on the 7th of July, 2005. She had the highest speed rating by 9 points, but was a 3 year old running against older horses. Going up in class. Most of the horses in the race had run in high price allowances races, and even some stake / handicap races. She ran second at very low odds.

Example Race #5

Here's a great example. The 6th race at Belmont; July 8, 2005. Karakorum Splendor was running in a 7-furlong allowance race. She was running in the same class as her last race – where she finished second. Dropping 1 pound, coming back in I month. She paid $4.40 – a great price considering her speed rating was a phenomenal nine points higher than the second horse.

Example Race #6

Here's an awesome bet! Souris, running in the 7th at Belmont, July 16, 2005. She is a five-year-old mare racing against four year olds and up. Last race, July 2, 2005. Going up two pounds, but shows she can carry the weight and win at the distance recently. Going down in class – from a graded stakes to a non-graded stake. Last race, lost by two lengths, came in second. Speed rating for last three races: 91. Next best horse: Cherry Bomb with an 81. That's a10 point spread! Souris paid an awesome $3.70!

Example Race #7

Bet of the month. Woodbine, July 17th 2005. 8th race. Wannatalkaboutme was running 51/2 furlongs. Last race: July 2, 2005. A two-year old filly racing against other two year olds. Running in the same class as previous week, but every other horse in the race was going up in class! Going up 1/2 furlong in distance. Won his last race against higher-class horses. Speed rating a phenomenal 16 points higher than second choice. That is amazing. What was more amazing: she paid $3.70. A horse with a 16-point higher speed rating should be 1 to 5.

Example Race #8

August 20, 2005. Eighth race at Delaware Park. 1 1/16 Mile on the Dirt. The bet: Separato. 2-1 in the morning line. Ran fourth last time out but finished within 1 ¾ lengths of the winner. Racing back at the same distance at previous race. 291 total speed rating for the last three races. Second best horse: Play Bingo 277 total speed rating. Going up one pound in weight, but shows the ability to carry more weight at the same distance within the pest 90 days. Dropping in class from a $100,000 stake race to a $55,000 stake race. Ran 34 days ago, but gets in due to a speed rating of three points or higher per race. Won and paid $5.00. A great price on a horse with a speed rating that much higher.

WARNING

If you love the action, love to bet, this system is not for you. I would suggest joining gamblers anonymous and seeing psychological help for your addiction.

This system is for people who desire to make money while minimizing their risk. Stay away from gamblers. Stay away from naysayers. Focus on the work you need to do. Treat it as a business, not a pastime. Do not allow others to wish you luck. Luck is needed by the ill-prepared, those ruled by their emotions, people who are dreamers rather than planners.

See you at the cashier's window.